The Treehouse Adventures of Nate-Nate & Maxie Dog

— • —

NOAH, the Ark, and the Animals

by S. Otwell

Cover Illustration by Leon Ducker Sr.

HIS Publishing Group
4310 Wiley Post Rd., Suite 201D
Addison, Texas 75001
info@hispubg.com

ISBN: 978-0-578-19713-5

The Treehouse Adventures of Nate-Nate & Maxie Dog:
Noah, the Ark, and the Animals /Shannon Otwell—1st ed.
10 9 8 7 6 5 4 3 2 1

Printed in the United States of America

To: *Nate-Nate*

From: *Daddy*

These stories are written about the adventures of a wonderful son and his dog as they dreamed of playing in a treehouse. Nate-Nate never had his own treehouse but these stories will remind us of what can be done when we use just a little bit of our imagination and dare to dream. Each person that reads these stories has the same capabilities as the characters in the story and can do great and awesome things. You see, as always it is not who we are or what we are but who is in us, and when we have Christ in our lives *nothing* is impossible.

One wet and soggy summer day, Nate-Nate and Maxie dog were lying around the house bored. You see, it had rained for quite a few days and the ground was wet and soggy. The two wanted to go out and play but there was nothing they could do as the rain seemed to keep coming. As Nate-Nate and Maxie dog sat at the kitchen bar and finished eating their lunch, they kept looking outside for a glimpse of hope. They were looking for a small break in the rain so that they could go outside and play. Then, as they were almost finished, they saw a small bright light shining through the window. This was what they needed, a little break in the rain and Mom would surely let them go outside and play.

After putting his dishes in the dishwasher, Nate-Nate went straight to his mom and asked her to go outside. She was reluctant at first but with a little bit of begging from Nate-Nate and Maxie dog, she allowed them to go outside. The rules were simple though—No Playing In The Rain! So, they would have to stay in the treehouse. Nate-Nate and Maxie dog made a handshake agreement and ran to put on their raincoats to go outside. As they were running out of the house, Maxie dog looked over at a pile of animals on the floor belonging to Nate-Nate. Maxie dog barked until Nate-Nate grabbed them and took them to play with. When they had everything they needed, they ran out the back door and with a *'swoosh'* they were in the treehouse.

When the two made it into the treehouse the first thing that they noticed was how wet the inside was. After dumping out a few quick pails of water and a quick mop of the area, they were ready to get down to business. You see, they knew that it was time to "drop the sails" and use their imaginations. With that, the two were off and headed for an adventure. The adventure this time was heading to a place where there was *No Rain!* Somewhere that was dry and where they could run and play without any mud puddles. Nate-Nate and Maxie dog remembered something about a man named Noah. They could not remember exactly what he did or why but that he *surely* lived in an area without rain. With the decision made they were headed off to meet the man named Noah.

Noah was a good man and highly thought of by God. The problem was they did not know how to find him. Back in those days, people did not have addresses or mailboxes. Also, there were no maps of the area showing where people lived. Finding Noah was going to be harder than they thought. All of a sudden there was a *'thud'* and without noticing Nate-Nate had flown the treehouse into a large house-like object. As Nate-Nate and Maxie dog got out of the treehouse they realized that they had not hit a house. Instead, they had hit a boat! This was no ordinary boat, though. This was a *huge* boat, bigger than anything they had ever seen!

Nate-Nate and Maxie dog were not sure where they were but they decided to climb down and check it out. As they climbed down through the inside of the boat, they noticed that there were lots of designated areas for animals. There was a large area for the elephants and a small area for skunks. There was even a medium size area for bears. As they walked through the different levels of the boat they figured there must be enough areas for almost every animal on the earth. Nate-Nate wondered if this was some new type of zoo where all of the animals would be kept and people could come and see them. While thinking about this and wandering around, they ended up coming to the door to exit.

oth Nate-Nate and Maxie dog were a little worried about stepping outside as they were not sure where they were. Also, they had bumped into this boat and the owner may be angry. As they stepped outside of the boat they quickly realized two things: (one) the boat was huge, and (two), they were in a very dry area. You see, there was dirt everywhere. In fact, it looked as if there had never been any rain in the area! They both wondered why anyone would build a boat in the middle of a dry area. Not knowing the answer to the question they decided to go and try to find someone that could help them. So, with that, they set off looking for some help.

After walking around for what seemed like an hour, they heard something that sounded like voices. They ran around the corner and there, swinging from the top of the boat, was a family working on building the remainder of the boat. The leader of the group was on the ground with a large set of building plans and he was telling the people what to do. The rest of the group was swinging like trapeze artist hammering, pasting, cutting, installing, and everything that needed to be done to build the boat. Then with a loud, *'WHAM'*, the last nail was installed. Out of the air came the workers as they all landed by the man with the plans. Then the man with the plans took a big, deep breath and said, "Wow, it is finished."

Nate-Nate walked up to the man and asked him, "Sir, what do you mean it is finished?" The man quietly folded the plans and put them in their case, then he gently grabbed his white beard and sat down. He turned and looked at Nate-Nate and asked him, "Why good man, whom may I ask are you?" Nate-Nate replied, "Oh, I am sorry sir. I am Nate-Nate and this is my dog, Maxie. We are the ones that landed the treehouse on the top of your boat and we are very sorry." The old man stood looking up and saw the treehouse on top of the boat. With that, he let out a large laugh, "HA"! "My good boy, my name is Noah and I am the builder of this large ark. How would you and your dog like to join us for dinner?"

Nate-Nate and Maxie dog looked at each other in surprise as they found their man, Noah, and now they were offered to eat dinner with him. "Mr. Noah, we would be honored to have dinner with you. "Can I ask what you are having?" replied Nate-Nate. With a loud laugh, Noah replied, "We are having a special doughnut pizza with a sprinkle of chips on top and fresh milk to drink." Nate-Nate and Maxie dog looked around and then nodded in agreement—they were all in for dinner! As they got to Noah's home and began to sit down for dinner, Noah called everyone together and asked for prayer. While he was praying for dinner he also asked a prayer for God to watch over them with the coming flood.

As everyone was eating and enjoying the time together at the table, Nate-Nate and Maxie dog were a little worried. They did not understand, what was this big flood Noah had prayed about? Nate-Nate finally got the courage up and asked Noah, "Mr. Noah, I see that you are building this big boat and all. The weather is really dry here and then you asked a prayer for the coming flood. I don't understand what is going on?" Noah sat back in his chair and looked deeply into Nate-Nate's eyes and said, "Son, I understand what you are asking me. A few years ago, God came and told me to build this ark and that he was going to bring a great flood to the earth. A flood which will cover the entire earth and the only way that we will survive is for us to build this ark."

"Mr. Noah, that is scary," said Nate-Nate, "why does God want to destroy the earth that he created?" "That is a very good question, Nate-Nate. You see, people have stopped listening to God. In fact, people are not listening to him at all and they have become very mean and ugly towards each other and towards him," said Noah. "Wow, that is not cool at all. I understand them not listening but I am not sure I like God destroying everything. What about the animals that are out there? What will happen to them?" asked Nate-Nate. "That is another great question; you see the ark has very specific sizes that God gave us. We are to put a male and female of every kind of animal on the ark with us so that after the flood they can start life over", Noah said. "I totally understand why the ark is so large now," Nate-Nate said, "but I am not sure about the destruction. I thought that God was a great and loving God, not mean."

"Oh, Nate-Nate, you see our God is a very loving God and he is not mean at all. When God created people, he made everything perfect but an evil angel wanted to be like God. He fell from heaven and he has been trying to get people to follow him instead of God. It hurts God so much that he can't stand to see what the people are doing, so he has chosen to start over. He has asked for my family to build this ark so that we can be part of his plan to start over," Noah said. Nate-Nate thought for a minute and then said to Noah, "That is terrible how people have turned away from God. Maxie dog and I would like to help you get the animals if you will let us." "That sounds like a great idea! In fact, we can start tonight and find the animals that are nocturnal. Tomorrow, many more animals will be coming and we will need all the help that we can to get them into the ark", said Noah.

With that, Nate-Nate and Maxie dog went off with Noah into the woods to find some animals. The rest of the family started putting the final touches on the areas where each animal would stay during their time on the ark. Each area had to have food for the animals and a nice space for them to lie down and sleep with a blanket to keep warm at night. Maxie dog led the way into the woods, as he used his nose to help find the animals that they needed. First, they found a few fire-flies. They put them into a jar to use as light to help them see the other animals. Next, were the squirrels and then a couple of opossum. Nate-Nate quickly saw two lizards which he grabbed and put on his shoulder so that they would not get hurt. Noah got a couple of rabbits and skunks, also. When their arms were full of creatures, they started to walk back to the ark. Then, some owls started flying behind them.

When they got back they noticed something—there were a bunch of animals waiting on them! There were lions, tigers, zebras, moose, hippos, and bears all laying around on the ground waiting for instructions. Noah stopped in his tracks, turned and looked at Nate-Nate and said, "Surely, the Lord is with us!" Nate-Nate glanced over at Noah and said, "Why don't you go and get the list to check the animals in and I will go and get them in line." With that, Nate-Nate was off. He ran and jumped on the back of the hippo like he was a cowboy in the Wild West. Maxie dog ran around the back and started barking and herding the animals to get them into line, one female and on male of each animal. Nate-Nate took out his favorite duck call that his uncle gave him and blew it as loud as he could. When he did this all the birds started coming from the sky.

As fast as Nate-Nate and Maxie dog could get the animals in, Noah was checking his list. His family was in the ark and they were trying to get all the animals into the areas that had been created for them. The skunks were to go by the window, the pigs in the middle, the birds in the rafters, and the snakes along the walls. There was a little bit of a problem when the giraffe couldn't raise his head, because of his long neck, but Maxie dog hit the window and the giraffe was able to stretch his head out. There they were—the animals, Noah's family, and Nate-Nate and Maxie dog all loaded and ready for the voyage. But, with all of the calculations and construction completed, just as God had instructed, one thing did not work out. The door was to be closed from the outside. It could be latched and kept closed from the inside but the door had to be pushed shut by someone from the outside.

As Noah and Nate-Nate stood at the door wondering what to do, they started to notice that the door began to move! As they stepped back the door got closer and closer until it was completely closed. They were all enclosed in the ark. Noah turned and looked up to the heavens and said, "Thank you Lord, for closing the door and for protecting my family." With that, the skies started to darken and a cool air came upon the earth. Then, the first drop, and the second, then more and more came. The rain was starting and it looked like it was going to be around for a while. Noah borrowed a marker from Nate-Nate and made a mark on the wall, marking "Day 1" of the rain. You see, he was not sure how long they would be in the ark but he wanted to keep track of how long the rain lasted.

After making his mark on the wall Noah went outside on the deck of the ark to see what was going on. He stood there for a few minutes and then ran back inside. As he came back in, he looked over at Nate-Nate and Maxie dog and told them that they had better go and get into their treehouse and head for home. The rain was not going to stop and the ark was about to start floating. Nate-Nate and Maxie dog did not know what to do. They wanted to help and stay there with Noah and his family but they wanted to listen and go home also. They agreed that it was best for them to head back home, so they ran to the top of the ark and jumped into the treehouse. Nate-Nate instructed Maxie dog to "drop the sails," then the two of them reached out the window and waved good-bye to Noah and his family.

When Nate-Nate and Maxie dog returned home, they grabbed their toys and ran into the house. "Mom! Mom! Where are you?" exclaimed Nate-Nate as he ran around the house looking for her. "I am in here," Mom said, "in the bedroom." "Mom! Mom! You won't believe where we just went. We met Noah and the ark and I rode a Hippo and there were snakes and tigers!" said Nate-Nate. "Hold on Nate-Nate, slow down a little bit, you were just out in the treehouse. What do you mean you met Noah? Who is Noah?" Mom asked. "Mom! Mom! You remember when we get into the treehouse we can go places. Well, this time we went and met Noah and he has this big ark with animals." Nate-Nate said. "Hold on, hold on! Now, let me get this straight. You went and met Noah from the Bible?" Mom asked.

"Ok, I understand now! You and Maxie dog went and met Noah and you learned about the flood and how his family was saved," said Mom. "Well, not exactly, you see, we did meet Noah and his family and we helped them get the animals into the ark but we had to leave when the heavy rain started. Can you help us understand what happened to Noah? How long were they on the ark and do you know if Noah and his family survived?" Nate-Nate asked. "Oh, Nate-Nate that sounds great. Why don't you and Maxie dog climb up here on the bed and we will finish the story? Now you said that you left when the rain was starting, correct?" asked Mom. "Yes ma'am, the ark was just about to start floating," said Nate-Nate. "Ok, you see, Noah and his family and the animals had to deal with rain for 40 days and nights. The rain never stopped and it was so great that the entire earth was covered. The tallest mountains on the earth were even covered," said Mom. "That is a lot of rain!" said Nate-Nate.

"Yes, Nate-Nate that was a lot of rain", said Mom. She told the rest of the story about how the rain went on for 40 days and nights. When there was a break in the clouds, Noah took a small dove and sent him out to see if there was any dry land. The dove returned with nothing. He waited seven more days and sent the dove out again. This time the dove returned with an olive branch in his mouth. Noah waited another seven days and sent the dove out again, and this time, the dove did not return. She told how Noah and his family waited for the waters to dry up and the ark to finally reach land again. While Mom was finishing the story, Nate-Nate started to look worried as he noticed the rain starting again outside. "Mom, what happens if it rains on us for 40 days? What will happen to all of the animals and people?" Nate-Nate asked. As Mom closed the Bible, she looked over at Nate-Nate and asked him to look out the window and tell her what he saw.

"Mom, all I see are a bunch of clouds, some rain, and a rainbow. Why is there a rainbow out there?" Nate-Nate asked. Mom paused for a minute and then said, "When Noah and his family were ready to get off the ark, God put a rainbow in the sky. The rainbow is God's promise that tells us he will never flood the earth again." Nate-Nate paused and said, "I never knew that was where the rainbow came from. That is so cool! So, every time I see a rainbow it is like God is talking to me." Mom replied, "That is true, Nate-Nate. God is talking to you every day. And just as he looked out after Noah, he will look out after you. You see, after Noah, his family, and all the animals got off the ark they started life again. You and I are descendants of his family." "Wow! Thank you, God, for choosing Noah, and thank you, Noah, for being a person that God could trust. I pray that I can be a person like Noah," said Nate-Nate.

With that, they all curled up together on the bed and took a long nap as the rain came down outside. Mom was dreaming of how great her son would be and how he could be like Noah. Maxie dog was dreaming of playing with the animals on the ark and sharing his dog bones with them. Nate-Nate was dreaming of getting back to the treehouse and what adventure would be next.

www.ingramcontent.com/pod-product-compliance
Lightning Source LLC
Chambersburg PA
CBHW042102060426

42446CB00046B/3471